COMPILED BY BISHOP CALVIN BETHEA

EXPERIENCE A NEW BEGINNING WORKBOOK

Blueprint for Building A Firm Spiritual Foundation & A Road Map For New Christians

God's Life
PUBLISHING

Published by God's Life Publishing
744 Chancellor Ave
Irvington, New Jersey 07111
973 373-4434

Printed in U.S.A.

God's Life Publishing is a ministry of God's Life Christian Church, and is dedicated to making resources available to the body of Christ in the form of printed publications and e-books. All resources has been tried in our local church and other churches before we publish them for the body of Christ.

Experience A New Beginning Workbook

ISBN-0991626303
ISBN-978-0-9916263-0-4

All scripture are taken from the King James Version
Rights for publication of this workbook in other languages are contracted by God's Life Publishing.

Cover Designed by
God's Life Publishing

For dealers and store locations or ordering information visit:
godslifepublishing.org
or send an email to:
godlife@aol.com

ABOUT THE AUTHOR

Bishop Calvin L. Bethea is known as a teacher of the believers' identity in Christ. As a result of his simplicity in teaching, he is able to reconcile multitudes, edify the saints and glorify God. Bishop Bethea is the senior pastor of **God's Life Christian Church** (*godslifeonline.org*) which he along with his wife Dr. Melrose founded in 1993. He is also the founder of **Insight For Leaders Ministerial Fellowship** that currently oversees churches locally in New Jersey, Pennsylvania and as far as Hawaii. He simply terms himself as a coach to pastors. Many today refer to him as a pastor's pastor. He is committed to using every gift, talent or skill to cause men to live a victorious life through Christ. He can be heard voicing the name of Jesus Christ through God's Life Christian Church television broadcast called "Living Waters" every Sunday on Comcast Cable. He lives and stands on 2 Corinthians 5:17, "Therefore if any man be in Christ, he is a new creature: old things are passed away; behold, all things are become new."

Bishop Bethea is a Vietnam Veteran, a publisher, a business owner (Christianwear House/King's Apparel & Supplies) a Commissioner on the Irvington Housing Authority and an adopted father to numerous children.

WORDS OF COMMENDATION

"Experience A New Beginning" is a very well written book in simple language, making it easy to understand. The lessons will teach the new born again believer what it means to be saved, and how to live a life pleasing to The Lord. It is a must read for all, and can help guide both young and old in The Lord."

Pastor Anthony Franks
Senior Pastor, Grace Redemption Ministries, Kaneohe, Hawaii

....

"For 18 years, I have witnessed Bishop Calvin Bethea come along side of many believers through the navigation of Holy Spirit. I believe this manual is birth from the many years that I have watch him work passionately with new believers from all walks of life. "Experience A New Beginning" will cultivate growth and establish a firm foundation for believers in the body of Christ."

Pastor Ron Burgess
Daily Application Ministries, Maplewood, NJ

....

"This booklet is an extremely valuable road map for the new believer to know what to do, what's next for them and how to navigate the challenges that come with a new life in Christ."

Reverend Daniel de Gracia, II
Columnist, Washington Times

....

When a person becomes a new believer in Christ, it is a necessity for them to establish a solid foundation in their faith. In the "Experience A New Beginning" by Bishop Calvin, new believers will receive instructions, truth and guidance from God's Word on how to build a solid foundation of their faith, how to become a strong believer and instructions from God's Word on how to face and overcome many of life's challenges and circumstances. As a new convert, you will appreciate and enjoy the easy to read format of the "Experience A New Beginning" workbook.

Rev. Todd Bailey
Todd Bailey Ministries, Fort Collins, Colorado

....

"Experience A New Beginning" is a useful practical tool to assist the new believer in establishing a Biblically sound foundation. Such a foundation is a vital step to living a committed life that pleases God."

Dr. Stephenia Burgess, DPM
Daily Application Ministries, Maplewood, NJ

....

"A essential training tool for every Pastor and every New Believer"

Rev. Dr Kevin E. Knight, Sr.
Senior Pastor Heavenly Temple COGIC, Jersey City, NJ

....

This study guide, by Bishop Calvin Bethea, is a valuable volume! It is valuable first because it contains instruction in the most important dimension of life: how to come to know God and how to walk with God, through Jesus Christ. It is valuable secondly because its contents are so practical, so plainly expressed, so "user-friendly"! I am impressed with the heart of a shepherd that motivates Bishop Bethea to ensure that God's sheep have a clear, pure understanding of the fundamentals of the doctrine of Christ. And I am convinced that not only Bishop Bethea's ministry, but many others, will benefit from this powerful discipleship tool!

Bishop Michael A. Blue
Senior Pastor, The Door of Hope Christian Church, Marion, SC

WORDS OF COMMENDATION

After an acute perusal of this work, "Experience A New Beginning", I can honestly say it will serve as a tremendous tool for gaining insight and understanding the how to(s) of walking out your faith according to the Holy Scriptures. We know that without fail, challenges will be faced by the believer but a clearer understanding is forged through usage of this guidebook. The new Christian now hold something in their hands that literally translates the precepts of the Word of God into a simple practical guide for their journey as they seek to live a life pleasing to God.

I believe if, as a new Christian, I had this it would have helped me learn the vocabulary of the Kingdom much sooner and helped me to mature in the things of God in a healthier fashion. Bishop Bethea, this work is a job well thought out and well done. So to every student of the Word, dig into this mine-field and you will find treasures. May your joy be full!

Bishop Carl E. Harris
Senior Pastor, Emmanuel Temple The House Of Praise, Waihiwa, Hawaii

"A good resource for counselors to make available to clients as part of their bibliotherapy. It provides succinct explanations and helpful study guide to knowing and following God; ultimately it invites a decision towards Christian maturity."

Bel DeGracia, DCC, PhD,
NCCA Licensed Clinical Christian Counselor, Honolulu, Hawaii

"A masterly, well-researched, easy to comprehend and gracefully written for new believers; lessons succeeds in bringing a lifetime foundation to one's Christian faith."

Reverend Dan de Gracia,
Chairman Emeritus & Chief Operating Officer,
Healthcare Management Organization, Honolulu, Hawaii

PREFACE

Experience A New Beginning

My favorite scripture that I live by is 2 Corinthians 5:17, *"Therefore if any man be in Christ, he is a new creature: old things are passed away; behold, all things are become new."*
This one verse has revolutionized my understanding of the believer's identity in Christ. It has led me to take advantage of every opportunity to teach others the Biblical truths as to who we are in Christ, what we have and how to walk daily in this new life.

"Experience A New Beginning" was birthed out of a new convert inquiring if there were study materials available to guide a new believer in foundational Biblical truths. I found many helpful books for new converts however, none met the school format this convert was seeking. Upon trying to assist this person, I became very disappointed that I could barely find a book or workbook that explained basic Christian doctrine. I found books that required the reader to have a prior biblical knowledge and books that required a Greek dictionary to interpret, read and understand the content. This began a journey to create a simple, basic, easy-to-read workbook with assignments to reinforce what was discussed.

The format of the workbook is to present a lesson, followed by a few questions and a verse of scripture to memorize. My goal with the memory verse was to select a verse of scripture that would serve as an overview of the entire teaching in that lesson.

Once this book was near completion, I provided copies to every member in the church that I pastored. Every Sunday after refreshments, we created a Bible School environment. I would present a lesson to this group of believers. They were required to study the next lesson for the following Sunday. At the end of the lessons, we had a review of the entire workbook; then we presented certificates to every participant.

I discovered that the new converts, the senior saints, the youths, the elders and the ministers could all understand and follow the simple format without struggle. No one felt intimidated by the materials or that the information was above or below their understanding. As we progressed through the lessons, the members became more excited, participation increased, memory verses were on their tongues and everyone had a sense of Spiritual growth. Most of all, everyone felt a sense accomplishment at the end.

Sensing a need for more in the Body of Christ to get the workbook, I began to send copies to fellow leaders, that play an instrumental role in the lives of other saints to review this compilation. The reviews were a sure sign that this workbook was a needed resource.

My prayer is that this workbook would become a much needed and utilized tool that would lay a proper doctrinal and spiritual foundation in the believer's life. This workbook, can be used by any denomination or any size group. This resource could also be used for new converts class, for personal study or Bible study classes.

I extend my heartfelt thanks to the members of God's Life Christian Church for partnering with me in testing and giving their input to make this workbook a valuable resource in the Christian's life. A special thanks to ministry leaders across the United States that reviewed this workbook and encouraged me to get it published for the benefit of the Body of Christ.

I want to acknowledge my wife Dr. Melrose Bethea for her never ending prayers, coaching and support to see this workbook to its completion.

I want to also thank one of my adopted daughters, Min. Margaret Adjoga-Otu, for demanding that these lessons be put in book form and be published.

GET THE MOST OUT OF THIS BOOK BY RECEIVING JESUS CHRIST AS LORD AND SAVIOR

If you are searching for Jesus and want to experience a new beginning through this workbook, then you must begin by accepting Jesus Christ as your personal Savior. You can pray the prayer below, thereby making this workbook a valuable tool in your eternal life. At anytime while using this workbook, you feel the need for assurance of your salvation you may refer to the prayer below.

God loves you no matter who you are, no matter your past. God loves you so much that He gave His only begotten Son for you. The Bible tells us that, *"whosoever believeth in him shall not perish, but have everlasting life"* (John 3:16). If you would like to receive Jesus Christ into your life, say a prayer similiar to the one below.

PRAYER OF SALVATION

Heavenly Father, I come to you admitting that I am a sinner. I know I have done many terrible things. I choose to turn away from all my sin, and ask you to cleanse me from all unrighteousness. I believe that Jesus is your Son and that He died on the cross for my sins. I also believe that He rose again on the third day from the dead so that I might be forgiven. I ask Jesus Christ to be my Lord and Savior today. I choose to follow and obey His word. I ask for the Holy Spirit to come into my life and guide and lead me into all truth. Thank you for saving me and making me your child. Amen!

If you prayed this prayer to receive Jesus Christ as your personal Lord and Savior for the first time, please email us at godlife@ aol.com. Immediately tell your family and friends. Get a Bible, begin to read the Gospel of John, find a local Bible believing church, complete the seven lessons in this workbook and grow in the grace of our Lord and Savior Jesus Christ.

EXPERIENCE A NEW BEGINNING

FOREWORD

My name is Apostle Michael Eugene Goings. I am the Senior and Founding Pastor of Outreach Family Fellowship, one church in two locations in Dillon and Florence, SC. Bishop Calvin Bethea served for several years under my tutelage. He proved himself to be a faithful and dependable servant, even serving for a time as one of my armor bearers. I have been blessed to watch him grow as a man of God who has now been pastoring his own flock for some time. I even had the honor of overseeing his installation service to the bishopric. Bishop Bethea is an established and seasoned messenger of the gospel who has demonstrated an assiduous methodology in his study of the scriptures.

I was elated, as I read through this treatise on lessons for the new believer, to see that his approach to making Kingdom principles straightforward and unpretentious was still intact. I whole heartedly recommend this exposition for any new converts and those even wishing to build the foundation of their faith and confession in Christ. It would also be beneficial for those who may be in the valley of decisions about making a choice towards salvation. The lessons contained in this study will serve as an essential guide to helping the new believer complete a successful transition during the infancy stage of development. It will also serve to dispel some common myths and misinformation in regard to what it means to become a follower of Christ. All of the teachings are very scripturally sound and actually will serve to refer the reader back to the holy writ. This guide offers quite relevant, applicable, and practical message to help believers establish a solid foundation in their relationship with Christ. Bishop Bethea makes it plain and simple so that anyone can understand the process of maturation as a Christian. I would recommend this dissertation to any pastor or ministry who is looking for a manual for new converts.

I have been in ministry for over forty years. and I must admit that this handbook has sparked something in me. Having served as a spiritual father to Bishop Bethea, I was moved uplifted, and quite pleased to see what God had presented through one of my progeny. I pray that this resource will be published and spread throughout the body of Christ to serve as a blessing to many.

APOSTLE MICHAEL EUGENE GOINGS, SENIOR & FOUNDING PASTOR
OUTREACH FAMILY FELLOWSHIP
DILLON & FLORENCE, SOUTH CAROLINA

LESSON TABLE OF CONTENTS

LESSON

1

The New Life

Salvation

"For by grace are ye save through faith; and that not of yourselves: it is the gift of God: Not of works, lest any man should boast."
(Ephesians 2:8-9)

THE NEW LIFE

This workbook consists of seven lessons designed to biblically guide the believer to living the life that would be pleasing to the Lord. These lessons will show that God has given Christians specific instructions as to how to live the very best life possible. As a believer, why not make a commitment to the Lord right now to complete each of these lessons. Thereby, these lessons will make you a student of God's word and a child of God committed to living for Christ.

THE SALVATION EXPERIENCE

You are a member of God's family because you received the Lord Jesus Christ as your personal Savior by faith. This has brought you into a wonderful and fulfilling relationship with God who created you. Receiving Christ as your Savior begins an eternal relationship with God. It is much more than just going to heaven when you die. Salvation is a gateway that begins your new life. Jesus said, *"I am come that they might have life, and that they might have it more abundantly"* (John 10:10b).

You must understand that you have been saved FROM sin.

Everyone in the family of God was a sinner saved by God's grace. *"For by grace are ye saved through faith; and that not of yourselves: it is the gift of God: Not of works, lest any man should boast"* (Ephesians 2:8-9).

I know that you want to live for the Lord and become the best Christian that you possibly can. This is why you are reading this workbook and taking this spiritual foundation course. May this always be your desire.

There are many truths in the Bible that will greatly help you to live the life that the Lord wants you to. This life is the best you could possibly have.

BEING "BORN AGAIN"

A person who receives Christ as their Savior and receives eternal life begins as a newborn baby in the Lord. Jesus told Nicodemus that to see the kingdom of God one must be "born again" *(See John 3:1-19)*. This is called the "new birth", and means a person has become a new member of the family of God. There is much to learn about the Lord. Now, you can learn about spiritual things of the Lord because you have received the new birth and been indwelled by the Holy Spirit of God.

INDWELLING OF THE HOLY SPIRIT

What does it mean that you are "indwelled" by the Holy Spirit of God?

Jesus in Acts 1:5, told his disciples that within a short time they would receive the "baptism of the Holy Spirit". He said, *"For John truly baptized with water; but ye shall be baptized with the Holy Ghost not many days hence."* Jesus told them this just before he returned to Heaven. In Acts 1:4, He said that they were to wait until they had received the Holy Spirit. In Old Testament times, those who believed in God did not permanently receive the indwelling of the Holy Spirit. Now, the Lord was going to do something new. All believers would receive the Holy Spirit, who would be with them forever. Please refer to the account of the disciples receiving the indwelling of the Holy Spirit in Acts 2:1-4. Since that day, all Christians have been able to received the indwelling of the Holy Spirit.

Jesus had promised the disciples earlier that He would send them the Holy Spirit to guide them in their lives. *"But the Comforter, which is the Holy Ghost, whom the Father will send in my name, he shall teach you all things, and bring all things to your remembrance, whatsoever I have said unto you"* (John 14:26).

Jesus also said, *"Howbeit when he, the Spirit of truth, is come, he will guide you into all truth: for he shall not speak of himself; but whatsoever he shall hear, that shall he speak: and he will shew you things to come. He shall glorify me: for he shall receive of mine, and shall shew it unto you"* (John 16:13-14). The Holy Spirit is God, living within us. He, the Holy Spirit is God and is identified as the third member of the Godhead, made up of the Father, Son and Holy Spirit.

THE BEGINNING OF THE CHURCH

When the Holy Spirit came in Acts chapter 2, the Lord Jesus began the church. Everyone who has been saved since the Day of Pentecost, became a member of the "Body of Christ". The Body of Christ is made up of all persons that are saved. The Bible uses the word "body" in the same sense that we do in referring to our human bodies. Our body is made up of all our body parts. Therefore, all of our body parts are referred to as one body. The local church is made up of a group of Christians, who are in fact a part of the whole body of Christ. Some refer to this as the "Universal Church" because all Christians are in it. The local church, which the Bible speaks the most about, is made up of a group of believers joined together in a small geographic location to serve the Lord. That is what your church is.

NOW YOU ARE ABLE TO UNDERSTAND THE BIBLE AND SPIRITUAL THINGS OF GOD

The indwelling of the Holy Spirit begins when a person believes in the Lord Jesus and is saved.

"Now we have received, not the spirit of the world, but the spirit which is of God; that we might know the things that are freely given to us of God. Which things also we speak, not in the words which man's wisdom teacheth, but which the Holy Ghost teacheth; comparing spiritual things with spiritual. But the natural man receiveth not the things of the Spirit of God: for they are foolishness unto him: neither can he know them, because they are spiritually discerned" (1 Corinthians 2:12-14).

Paul further says, *"What? know ye not that your body is the temple of the Holy Ghost which is in you, which ye have of God, and ye are not your own?"* (1 Corinthians 6:19).

THE HOLY SPIRIT IS OUR HELPER TO UNDERSTAND THE BIBLE

Because the Holy Spirit lives within us, He gives us the "new nature", which is the nature of God. We are now able to understand spiritual things because the Holy Spirit working in us helps us to do so.

THE OLD NATURE

Before a person is saved he or she does not have the nature of God. This person has what the Bible refers to as the "old" or "carnal" nature. That is why we sin. Our carnal nature is the nature of rebellion and rejection of God, which is sin. It came when Adam and Eve yielded to Satan's temptation and sinned.

Because a person who has not received Christ only has the old carnal nature, he cannot please God. *"Because the carnal mind is enmity against God; for it is not subject to the law of God, nor indeed can be. So then, those who are in the flesh cannot please God"* (Romans 8:7-8).

Note what else Paul said, *"Wherefore, as by one man sin entered into the world, and death by sin; and so death passed upon all men, for that all have sinned"* (Romans 5:12).

Sin is the reason things in the world are not as they should be. God intended that mankind would live a peaceful, satisfying and abundant life. Man has not done what God intended because of the presence of sin; sin has caused all the grief and sorrow we see today.

Sin is rebelling against God by not living as we should. Our loving Creator, God, wants the best for us. God's commandments are given so we would know what is best for us. It is the same thing that a loving parent does for his or her child. The parent instructs the child not to do certain things that are harmful to him or her. If the child rebels and does them anyway, he are she will be hurt. Sin is therefore the destructive thing which cause us harm.

One of the problems with sin is that it can give pleasure for a time. For example a child who loves to play in the street considers it fun. Because it is fun; there is a drive to go straight there each time the child is allowed out-doors. Although it seem fun to be there, it is a deadly place to play. Many of the vices we are familiar with such as smoking, drinking, doing drugs and gambling (to name only a few) do give pleasure. Nevertheless, the pleasure distracts us from the reality of its deadly effects.

As a child of God the Bible says to put away the destructive things out of your life. Paul told the Colossians to "mortify", meaning "put to death", sin within our lives (See Colossians 3:5-17).
To the Romans he said, *"Let not sin therefore reign in your mortal body, that ye should obey it in the lusts thereof. Neither yield ye your members as instruments of unrighteousness unto sin: but yield yourselves unto God, as those that are alive from the dead, and your members as instruments of righteousness unto God. For sin shall not have dominion over you: for ye are not under the law, but under grace"* (Romans 6:12-14).

THE HOLY SPIRIT AT WORK IN OUR LIVES

Because the believer is indwelled by the Spirit of God, we have the nature or desire to do as God wants. This is ultimately best for us. Thereby, we now have the ability to live as we should and as God intended. We can over-come sin and the temptation that comes from our old carnal nature. Because God lives within us, we can con-quer sin in our lives.

God's promise to the believer is that:
"There hath no temptation taken you but such as is common to man: but God is faithful, who will not suffer you to be tempted above that ye are able; but will with the temptation also make a way to escape, that ye may be able to bear it" (1 Corinthians 10:13).

This verse gives us great encouragement to know we can overcome sin in our lives. It is a life long process as the opportunity to sin is always present, this journey is a life long process. Be assured that as time goes by, you will by God's help, overcome sins in your life. Each sin overcome and each temptation refused is another step toward spiritual maturity. In time as you mature, by living for the Lord, these sins that may give you so much trouble now will bother you very little as you grow.

We should then look at each temptation that comes our way as but an opportunity to advance one more step toward a happier more fulfilling life. While triumphing over each temptation as it comes, we grow stronger and are better able to conquer it the next time it is brought to mind.

HAVING A BETTER UNDERSTANDING OF SALVATION

Having the Holy Spirit to guide us and help us understand the truths of the Bible even help us to better understand how we were saved. Few Christians begin their lives in Christ knowing all of what the Bible teaches about salvation. At first, people know in their hearts that they are sinners; then they reach out to the Lord in faith, trusting in His promise to save them.

As time goes on you will learn more about God, the Lord Jesus and salvation. The Bible says, *"Whom shall he teach knowledge? and whom shall he make to understand doctrine? them that are weaned from the milk, and drawn from the breasts. For precept must be upon precept, precept upon precept; line upon line, line upon line; here a little, and there a little"* (Isaiah 28:9-10).

These verses tell us that the principles *(truths)* of God are learned in time through study. We learn one principle, and that helps us to learn another one. All the truths of Scripture are tied together and the more we read and learn, the better we will be able to understand each truth.

Having the Holy Spirit living within us, gives the Christian a great deal of comfort. God is always with us. No matter what comes our way, we know God, working through the Holy Spirit, will guide us through (Read Romans 8:28).

A REVIEW OF THE THINGS WE KNOW ABOUT SALVATION

1. A person must realize he is a sinner.

Romans 3:23 says, *"For all have sinned and come short of the glory of God."* Before a person is saved, he must first realize he is a sinner and needs to be saved. We are born into sin and must be "born again".

2. A person must realize without salvation he will go to hell.

Romans 6:23 says, *"For the wages of sin is death; but the gift of God is eternal life through Jesus Christ our Lord."* This death is not only physical death but spiritual as well. The Bible says, *"And death and hell were cast into the lake of fire"* (Revelation 20:14). Had you died before trusting the Lord Jesus as your Savior, you would have experienced the second death, which is eternal separation from God in the Lake of Fire. Nevertheless, praise the Lord! Now you will never have to worry about Hell again, because God has saved you and given you eternal life. God promises, *"That whosoever believeth in him should not perish, but have eternal life. For God so loved the world, that he gave his only begotten Son, that whosoever believeth in him should not perish, but have everlasting life"* (John 3:15-16).

3. A person must believe that Jesus died for them and rose again.

Romans 5:8 says, *"But God commendeth his love toward us, in that, while we were yet sinners, Christ died for us."* Do not forget that we as sinners were condemned, but Jesus was not! He is the Son of God who never sinned or could sin because He is God. Moreover, God came to this earth and took our sins on Himself because we as sinners could not save ourselves. He died in our place and took our punishment (See Isaiah 53, 1Peter 2:24). He arose on the third day according to the Word of God (See 1Corinthians 15:3-4, Romans 5:18).

4. A person must confess Christ as Lord & Savior and receive Him into his or her heart.

Romans 10:9 say, *"That if thou shalt confess with thy mouth the Lord Jesus, and shalt believe in thine heart that God hath raised him from the dead, thou shalt be saved."*

This decision to be saved was not to join the church, be baptized or even change your way of living. What saved you was asking Jesus Christ, by faith, to come into your heart and be your Lord and Saviour. Baptism and church membership follow receiving Christ as your Savior, and have no part in God forgiving you and giving you eternal life.

YOUR ASSURANCE OF SALVATION

Now that you are saved, God wants you to have the assurance that your sins have all been forgiven. You are not saved when you get to heaven, but you are saved right now and for all eternity to come. John 3:36 says, *"He that believeth on the Son hath everlasting life...."* Hath means right now, and everlasting means forever and forever.

Jesus died for all your sins, even the ones you have not yet committed. Some Christians who are lacking in spiritual growth do not have this blessed assurance. John 10:27-28 says the following: *"My sheep hear my voice, and I know them, and they follow me: And I give unto them eternal life; and they shall never perish, neither shall any man pluck them out of my hand."* 1 John 5:13 says, *"These things have I written unto you that believe on the name of the Son of God; that ye may know that ye have eternal life, and that ye may believe on the name of the Son of God."*

Please remember the following; do not base your salvation on how you feel. Feelings can change from day to day, but God`s word remains the same (Matthew 24:35). A good feeling may be good, but it is not necessary to be saved. Did you know that the Bible never said you must have a feeling when you get saved? You are saved because you have done what the Bible says and God has declared you as one of His children.

There are some things that might cause you to doubt and not have the assurance God wants you to have.

1. **Always thinking about your past life can cause doubt.** God has forgiven all your sins and has forgotten them. He also wants you to forget them. Forget the past! It is all under the atoning blood of Christ (Isaiah l:18, Psalm 103:12).

2. **Wondering if God really received you causes doubts.** When you come to the Lord with a desire to be saved and asked Him to save you, you can be sure He did. Why? God, who cannot lie, has promised to. Just take Him at His word. John 6:37 says, *".... him that cometh, to me I will in no wise cast out."*

3. **Basing your salvation upon feelings or emotion causes doubts.**
Don't forget: feelings change - but the Bible, which is God's eternal word never does.
Read: Ephesians 2:8 and Romans 5:1 — **FAITH** - Assures - **NOT** feelings.

4. Trust God: Live as He commands - you will have assurance.
a.1 John 2:3. Do you really want to obey?
b. Romans 7:15-25. A War is going on.

LESSON SUMMARY

INSTRUCTIONS: This sheet is a review of the Biblical Truths found in this lesson. After each lesson answer the review questions. Look back in the lesson for the answers.

MY TESTIMONY

I received the Lord Jesus Christ as my personal Savior on _____ (date)

At_____(location).

Person/s who helped lead me to Christ were:

(Names)_____.
Pray that they continue to be an evangelist for Christ.

Write out Ephesians 2:8, 9

_____

_____

_____

_____

_____

Now memorize the scripture text. In doing so you will retain more of the lesson.

QUESTIONS:

1. *Romans 3:23 tells me that all people have* _____.

2. *Romans 10:9 tells me that I must confess* _____.

3. *I know I am saved because* _____.

4. *John 10:28 tells me God has given to me* _____.

5. *Name one thing that might cause you to doubt.* _____

_____

6. *Can you overcome all sin in your life?* _____ *What verse teaches this?* _____.

7. *When did the church begin?* _____. *(verse, day or place)*

8. *What is the Holy Spirit living within us called?* _____.

9. *Can lost people live for the Lord?* _____

Why? _____

10. *Write down a good verse that teaches assurance of salvation?* _____.

_____

_____

_____

_____

_____

_____

_____

~NOTES~

~NOTES~

LESSON

2

Your Responsibilities As A Child Of God
Adoption

"I beseech you therefore, brethren, by the mercies of God, that ye present your bodies a living sacrifice, holy, acceptable unto God, which is your reasonable service. And be not conformed to this world: but be ye transformed by the renewing of your mind, that ye may prove what is that good, and acceptable, and perfect, will of God."
(Romans 12:1-2)

YOUR RESPONSIBILITIES AS A CHILD OF GOD

Now that you are saved and have this assurance from the Word of God. God wants you to continue on in your Christian life. Remember Ephesians 2:8, 9 tells you that you were saved *"by grace through faith"* and not by good works you have done or ever will do.

After a person is saved, he becomes a new creature in Christ (2 Corinthians 5:17) and all things become new. As a result, you now have a desire to do what is right and the spiritual ability to live a godly life because you have God's Spirit or new nature. We are being obedient to God's Word when we obey and allow the Holy Spirit to direct us. Ephesians 5:18 tells the Christian, *"And be not drunk with wine, wherein is excess; but be filled with the Spirit."* To be filled with the Spirit means to allow Him to direct and be the guiding influence in our lives. As a new Christian you will want to do things that please the Lord. Let's look at several of the first things we need to do as a new Christian to fulfill our responsibilities to the Lord.

PUBLIC PROFESSION OF YOUR FAITH

Let family, friends and other people know that you have been saved. You should not be ashamed of Christ (Romans 1:16). It will also strengthen you in the Lord, because as you obey and do what the Bible instructs, you will grow and mature as a Christian. It is like a child who begins to attend school in the first grade. The teacher instructs the child in learning the alphabet. If the child obeys and learns them, he or she will soon begin to read. Maturing in Christ is similar. God's word is our textbook to teach us how we should live. It tells us how to live the best life we possibly can. As we obey the commandments of the Lord, we will internalize them and go on to learn other lessons. As a new Christian you should seek to obey the Bible, God's instruction book on life. The more obedient you are the faster you will mature in Christ.

BAPTISM AND CHURCH MEMBERSHIP

Jesus gave the disciples some instructions just before He ascended back to heaven as recorded in Matthew 28:19-20, *"Go ye therefore, and teach all nations, baptizing them in the name of the Father, and of the Son, and of the Holy Ghost: Teaching them to observe all things whatsoever I have commanded you: and, lo, I am with you alway, even unto the end of the world. Amen."* The word "teach" in verse 19 mean to disciple or win the lost to Christ. After a person is saved, the second thing he is instructed to do is be baptized (verse 19). Since the beginning of the first church, believers have given evidence of their faith in Christ by being baptized in water. Baptism occurs when a person is immersed under the water as a picture or symbol of the death, burial and resurrection of Christ.

BAPTISM - In the Bible, baptism always comes after a person has been saved. Baptism does not save you or keep you saved. It is an act of obedience to Christ and pictures what has already taken place in your heart. It describes our union with Christ as seen in Romans 6:3-5. Every Christian should be baptized soon after receiving Christ as Savior. Have you been obedient to Christ and been baptized?

In Acts 2:41, we find that when a person was saved, he was baptized and joined the local church. This baptism identifies you with the body of Christ and the local church. The church is God's place for Christians to be taught the Bible, to have fellowship with other Christians, and a place to pray and worship the Lord. Nothing can replace the church, not even Sunday morning T.V. or radio preaching. You need to be in church! You should immediately be baptized and join the local church after being saved. This is one of your first opportunities to obey the Lord and please Him.

CHURCH ATTENDANCE

Hebrews 10:25 tells us to be faithful in our church attendance. This means you should attend church as often as you are able. It is understandable that if a person is working or sick they cannot attend. However, unless by divine providence you are hindered you should attend church. Today, many believers ignore Bible Study Class. They feel content to attend only on Sunday Morning. Each service and meeting the church has is designed to help and aid the Christian in living abundant lives in Christ. In the Sunday morning service there will be in some cases more visitors, and generally lost people in church. The messages tend to be more evangelistic and the subject is generally geared toward salvation and edification.

The Sunday School and Bible Study is attended by the faithful members of the church and born again Christians, so the teachings are focused on helping them to grow in the Lord. Church members, who only attend the Sunday Morning services miss a great opportunity to receive the deeper spiritual truths of the Bible. You see, faithful attendance will be a key to your Christian life and growth. Support the special services as much as possible with your attendance. The last part of the Lord's instructions to the disciples in Matthew 28 instructs us to teach new converts the Word of God. This is done through the ministry of the local church in each of its services. Your Pastors are faithful in being on duty, prepared to teach and preach God's Word to help you grow in Christ. Your privilege is to attend and avail yourself of the opportunity.

One note on preaching and teaching. Many Pastors really pray and seek God's guidance in what to preach. They study really hard and spend a great deal of time in preparing their lessons and messages. It is estimated that most good pastors spend from four to six hours on each message. Being lead of the Lord, they come and deliver God's message to the church. However, if church members are not there they do not hear what God has to say to them as a local church.

When you choose not to attend Sunday Service, Bible Study and Prayer meetings you in fact are voting to discontinue them. You also are telling your neighbors and others in the church you do not think that these services are important. You will also miss the opportunity to show your love, and dedication to the Lord by not faithfully supporting the total ministry of the church. To be sure, it takes time, effort and expense to attend all the services of the church; However, let's make a reasonable effort. The benefits received will outweigh any sacrifices on your part.

One verse of Scripture that instructs how dedicated to the Lord we should be is found in Romans 12:1-2.

"I beseech you therefore, brethren, by the mercies of God, that ye present your bodies a living sacrifice, holy, acceptable unto God, which is your reasonable service. And be not conformed to this world: but be ye transformed by the renewing of your mind, that ye may prove what is that good, and acceptable, and perfect, will of God" (Romans 12:1-2).

THE LORD'S SUPPER

The Lord's Supper and baptism are two ordinances of the church. The Lord's Supper is also only for the saved person. 1 Corinthians 11:23-26 tells us what it represents. The bread represents Christ's body and the wine represents His shed blood for us. This is a reminder of what Christ has done for us until He comes back. Moreover, this is a serious time and should never be taken lightly.

GIVING TO THE LORD

1. Giving Yourself

Paul says in Romans 12:1, we should , ". . . present your bodies a living sacrifice, holy, acceptable unto God, which is your reasonable service." The Lord wants YOU more than anything else you might want to give to Him. Surrender yourself totally to Him by determining to follow and obey His word. Let Christ have control of your life.

2. Giving Your Praise and Thanksgiving

Giving is an act of worship. Hebrews 13:15 tells us to offer to God our praise for all that He has done for us. We praise Him with our lips through prayer and telling others about what Christ has done for us.

3. Giving of our Money & Possessions

Second Corinthians 9:7, tells us that God loves a cheerful giver. God told His people in the Old Testament to give into His storehouse. A reasonable offering is at least 10% of what you earn or receive. This is a matter between you and the Lord. God promised to bless those who give to His work (Malachi 3). In the New Testament, His word about faithful consistent giving with cheerfulness is confirmed. First Corinthians 16:2 gives us an example, to give of every increase (*whether it's $1 or $50,000*), to the local church as God has prospered. Stop right here and read 2 Corinthians 9:6-8. Believe what God says about His blessing for you and then obey Him every Sunday. This also is another way of expressing to the Lord your love and thanks.

God wants you to grow spiritually and become a mature Christian. Some Christians have a real struggle with making the commitment to give to the Lord. Christians who have been obedient understand the value of regular giving of offerings on all increases to the Lord. Note: As you read 2 Corinthians 9:7, it says, *"Every man according as he purposeth in his heart, so let him give; not grudgingly, or of necessity: for God loveth a cheerful giver."* You should make it a matter of prayer as to how much you are to give the Lord. Surely, it should be at least ten percent, as was required in the Old Testament. However, you may want to give more. Remember what verse 6 says, "But this I say, He which soweth sparingly shall reap also sparingly; and he which soweth bountifully shall reap also bountifully (2 Corinthians 9:6).

This is a matter between you and the Lord. A husband and wife should discuss the matter and pray about it together. If you have a spouse that is unsaved, and has no regular income, you should give from what you receive.

The same applies to children who are saved with unsaved parents. It is a good idea for the parent to instruct the child in Scriptural giving from their allowance or money they earn from chores. Remember, this is a matter between you and the Lord. It is a matter of exercising faith in the Lord to supply your needs. God has promised to meet your needs and to bless you materially when you faithfully give (Read Philippians 4:10-19).

David understood this principle and wrote, *"I have been young, and now am old; yet have I not seen the righteous forsaken, nor his seed begging bread"* (Psalms 37:25).

"Give, and it shall be given unto you; good measure, pressed down, and shaken together, and running over, shall men give into your bosom. For with the same measure that ye mete withal it shall be measured to you again" (Luke 6:38).

The money you give to the church pays the utility bills, buys literature, maintains the building, supports our outreach efforts and pays for the ministry of the church including the pastor's financial support. When some of the members of the church do not give on a consistent basis, these material expenses of the church can be neglected. A church will not have to pinch pennies, neglect missions, scrimp on purchasing literature or not properly support their pastor if all the members give. God will supply the need but only through those who faithfully give and let themselves be used as a channel to carry out God's work in the local church.

Write out Romans 12:1-2 and mark it in your Bible.

_____

_____

_____

_____

Memorize these verses.

QUESTIONS

1. What does Romans 10:11 tell us to do? _____

_____.

2. Does baptism and church membership save you? _____

_____.

3. Does God want you to be baptized after you have been saved? _____.

Have you been baptized? _____

EXPERIENCE A NEW BEGINNING

4. What Bible verse in Hebrews tells us to attend church and not forsake the assembling of ourselves?

_____

5. In the Lord's supper;
What does the bread represent? _____.

What does the wine represent? _____.

6. What are 3 things a Christian should give to the Lord?
_____.

7. Read Luke 6:38, again. What do you think that the phrase, " *For with the same measure that ye mete withal it will be measured to you again*", means? _____

_____

_____

_____

8. In the Scripture you read in Philippians 4:10-19, Paul told the Christians that, "God would supply all their needs."

Write down why you think it was important to share this with them?

_____

_____

_____

_____

_____

_____

_____

_____

~NOTES~

~NOTES~

LESSON

3

You And Your Bible

Spiritual Food

*"All scripture is given by inspiration of God,
and is profitable for doctrine, for reproof,
for correction, for instruction in righteousness:
That the man of God may be perfect,
thoroughly furnished unto all good works."
(2 Timothy 3:16,17)*

YOU AND YOUR BIBLE

The Bible is God's Word to man. It reveals the plan of God for all of mankind, the nature of God, the sinfulness of man, the plan of salvation in Christ, the prospects of heaven for the saved, the doom of the unsaved in hell and guidelines for the Christian to follow in order to live and act as he should. It is God's word to US. It is the most important object we have on this earth. We are to love it, learn it, and then live by it.

HOW WE GOT THE BIBLE
God has communicated with man in many different ways. Men like Joseph and Daniel of the Old Testament had dreams from God. Men like Isaiah and Ezekiel had visions from the Lord. In the Old Testament God also spoke quite a bit to people through His prophets.

But today, in New Testament times, God also speaks through His Word, the Bible. Hebrews 1:1-2 tells us that God spoke in many different ways in time past, but has in these last days spoken to us by His Son, who is called in the Bible, *THE WORD OF GOD* (See John 1:1 and Revelations 19:13).

God used several individuals over many years to record His word. In fact, God supervised His writing through these men of God. Even though men are not perfect, God did not allow these men to make errors when recording His word for the generations to follow. **The Holy Spirit directed these men. It was not just their ideas and thoughts.**

Second Peter says in 1:21, *"For the prophecy came not in old time by the will of man: but holy men of God spake as they were moved by the Holy Ghost.* In 2 Timothy 3:16-17 says, "All scripture is given by inspiration of God, and is profitable for doctrine, for reproof, for correction, for instruction in righteousness." Every word and every thought in the Bible is put there and approved by God Himself.

God has preserved His Word down through the years so we could have it to live by. The critics have tried to destroy it, but they have failed. In Matthew 24:35 it says, God's word will always stand, never to be done away with. God is the author of the Bible, and He has given it to us.

IMPORTANCE OF THE BIBLE TO YOU

God puts great emphasis on His Word. In fact, the longest chapter in the whole Bible (Psalm 119) speaks entirely about the Bible and its place in our life. God wants to talk with us and teach us. Second Timothy 3:16 tells us that all scripture is "inspired" of God and is profitable to us. This is called the doctrine of the "inspiration of Scripture." It means every word that the writer wrote was exactly what God wanted written. This is also called the doctrine of "verbal plenary inspiration"; in other words, every word was inspired of God and was without error.

"All scripture is given by inspiration of God, and is profitable for doctrine, for reproof, for correction, for instruction in righteousness: That the man of God may be perfect, thoroughly furnished unto all good works" (2 Timothy 3:16,17).

1. THE BIBLE IS OUR FOOD

The Bible is spiritual food to the Christian and is absolutely necessary if you are to grow and develop into a strong and mature Christian. We must have physical food to live and spiritual food to stay healthy spiritually. A new believer in Christ is called in the Bible a spiritual babe.
Peter tells us that new babes in Christ are to desire the sincere milk of the word that they might grow thereby (1 Peter 2:2). The only way a baby can develop and grow to adulthood is to eat properly. A Christian needs to eat from the Bible every day. A baby is not fed once or twice a week but has to be fed constantly.

2. THE BIBLE IS OUR LIGHT

The Bible is called a light, because it guides our daily walk with God. It tells us what to do and how to live. David said in Psalm 119:105, "Thy word is a lamp unto my feet, and a light unto my path." The Word of God and the Holy Spirit gives us direction.

3. THE BIBLE IS OUR SPIRITUAL WEAPON

Ephesians 6:11-17 says, we are to put on the whole armor of God that we might stand against the tricks of the devil. When Jesus was tempted by Satan, He met every temptation with God's Word (Matthew 4:3-11). We can do the same. The Bible is our sword in the battle against Satan's temptations. Psalm 119:11 says, "Thy word have I hid in mine heart, that I might not sin against thee."

HOW TO STUDY THE BIBLE

Since the Bible is God's Word to us, and He is the author, then we must read and study it, so that our spiritual sensitivity may be sharpened. The Bible is very important to us and is very profitable to us. We must therefore study it and live by it. There are different ways to feed on God's word in order to grow spiritually.

1. STUDY THE BIBLE BY HEARING IT

Romans 10:17 says, "**faith** cometh by hearing and hearing by the Word of God". We need this faith in order to live properly for the Lord. One of the best ways to study the Bible is to hear it preached and taught at church. That is why it is so important to be in church as much as possible. Another way is to read it out loud to yourself when you can. We can convince ourselves better than anyone else can when we hear our own voice speaking God's word.

2. STUDY THE BIBLE BY READING AND MEDITATING ON IT
Paul told us in 1 Timothy 4:13 to, "*. . . give attendance to reading, to exhortation, to doctrine.*" Every Christian should set aside a time everyday of their life to read the Bible. When we read the Bible, God is speaking to us. The best time to read the Bible is the first thing in the morning. Get up a little earlier so you can spend some time with the Lord in reading His word. We must do more than just read the Bible, we must also study the Bible. Think about what you are reading.

As a new Christian, don't expect to understand all you read. It may not all seem to make sense at first, but if you are patient and sincerely study, you will find the Bible fits together. A casual or brief glance once or twice a week, will not teach you the Bible. As you read, underline verses in the Bible that are special to you. Keep a small notebook beside you when you read and write down thoughts the Lord gives you. Have a Bible reading schedule and mark it as you read.

Write out and memorize Psalm 119:11

_____

_____

_____

READ YOUR BIBLE EVERY DAY !

QUESTIONS:

1. God speaks to mankind today primarily in visions and dreams. TRUE/FALSE

2. What verse in the Bible says God speaks through His Son? _____.

3. Give a Bible verse that refers to Jesus Christ as "The Word of God". _____

4. How many individuals did God use to write the Bible? _____

5. What is a verse that teaches "verbal plenary inspiration"_____.

6. What does verbal plenary inspiration mean? Circle your answer below:
   a. God inspired the writers of the Bible.

   b. Every word that they wrote was without error.

   c. Both of the above.

7. The longest chapter in the Bible is _____.

   What is the entire chapter about? _____.

8. Do you think that God wants you to read the Bible everyday? _____Yes _____No

Why should you? _____

~NOTES~

~NOTES~

LESSON

4

Prayer

Communication

*Let us therefore come boldly
to the throne of grace, that we may
obtain mercy and find grace
to help in time of need."
(Hebrews 4:16)*

PRAYER

After a child is born, he must have proper food to begin to grow. What a joy for those parents when he begins to walk. They look forward to that day when they will hear their baby say words like "da da" and "ma ma". This is sweet to the ears of a parent. So it is with the new born Christian. The Christian needs spiritual food, the Bible. He will begin to walk with God as he grows. It also delights the heart of God when His children talk to Him and call His name. This is what we call prayer. Prayer is talking to God as a child would talk to his natural father.

PRAYER IS A PRIVILEGE

We can come to God as our Father and expect Him to hear our requests because the new Christian is a child of God. As a member of God's family, we are expected to exercise this privilege by presenting our praise, thanksgiving and petitions to our Heavenly Father.

Hebrews 4:14-16 tells us of this wonderful privilege. All born-again Christians, can claim this promise.

"Seeing then that we have a great High Priest who has passed into the heavens, Jesus the Son of God, let us hold fast our profession. For we do not have a High Priest who cannot be touched with the feeling of our infirmities, but was in all points tempted like as we are, yet without sin. Let us therefore come boldly to the throne of grace, that we may obtain mercy and find grace to help in time of need" (Hebrews 4:14-16).

A song writer wrote: "What a friend we have in Jesus, All our sins and grief's to bear! What a privilege to carry everything to God in prayer..."

PRAYER IS POWERFUL

James 5:16b says, *"...The effectual fervent prayer of a righteous man availeth much."*
This simply means that when we pray as God wants us to, our prayers affect the way things happen and the way God does things. Even though God knows all things, He still desires us to pray. He delights to hear and answer our requests. All of us have things we should pray about. Prayer can do anything that God can do. Prayer is a powerful weapon against the enemy.

Solomon prayed for wisdom and became one of the wisest men to live. Elijah prayed and fire fell from heaven at Mt. Carmel. He also prayed that it would not rain for 3 years and it didn't. Daniel prayed and God delivered him from a den of lions. The church prayed in Acts 12 that Peter would be delivered from jail. While the group was praying, Peter was delivered and came to the door of the house where they were assembled. We can see numerous accounts of prayers being answered. An example of the power of prayer was seen in the life of George Muller. He operated a children's home with no financial backing and prayed in several hundred thousand dollars over the years to finance the home.

Have you ever prayed for something and received it? If you are saved, you prayed that Christ might come into your heart and save you, AND HE DID !! But don't forget the small things God gives to you in answer to prayer.

HOW DO I GO ABOUT PRAYING AS I SHOULD?

Many people want to know HOW I am suppose to pray? Don't feel badly if you are asking this same question. The disciples also had to come to Jesus and say, "Lord, teach us to pray"(Luke 11:1). Don't forget that praying is talking to God with a sincere heart. Talk with God as you would your natural Father, humbly, respectfully and sincerely. He is your Heavenly Father who has saved you from your sin.
Approach God boldly, but also in a respectful way, realizing He is Holy and Righteous. Don't be afraid, for He loves you and wants to have two way conversation with you.

Take time everyday to get alone with God and pray. This is a good time for your daily devotion in the Bible. Before studying, pray to the Lord. Just be honest and tell God what is on your heart and let him know you desire to hear what's on his heart as well. Express how you feel and what you desire.

Some people have begun as a new Christian to follow a simple rule of praying. You don't have to follow this exact pattern, but it might help you to develop a good pattern for praying. Make sure it doesn't become mechanical, God is REAL and your praying should be real.

ACTS:

A = Adore and worship the Lord first in praying.

C = Confess any sin and disobedience in your life and ask forgiveness.

T = Thank the Lord for all He has done for you, not only in salvation but for daily things.

S = Supplication, which means praying for the needs of others and yourself.

PROBLEMS IN YOUR PRAYER LIFE

Don't get discouraged at times when you pray and there is no immediate answer. Many people get discouraged and stop praying. If you are in fellowship with God, you can be sure that God has heard your prayer. God answers prayer in one of three ways: Yes; No; and Wait!

Many people have a problem with sin in their lives. A Christian's prayer can be hindered if he has unconfessed sin in his life. Psalm 66:18 says, *"If I regard iniquity in my heart, the Lord will not hear me."* God's word in James 5:16 says, *"The effectual fervent prayer of a righteous man availeth much."* We should not expect God to answer our prayers if we are not living as we should. Being "righteous", means being "right." God does not have to bless us when we are disobedient.

He does, however answer our prayer of confession of sin and seeks to restore us to fellowship. The problem with unconfessed sin in ones life is that it places a barrier between us and God. The barrier is not placed there by God, but by us when we sin. God says confess your sins, ask for forgiveness and He will forgive. He has promised to forgive and cleanse you from your sin if you confess them (1John 1:9).

You cannot overcome any sin that you refuse to confess. That is why confession is important. When we say that sin is sin we put it in its proper place. When we openly confess sin it puts us in a position to be set free from it.

Let's consider a few more important things about prayer that will help eliminate problems in your prayer life.

l. You must ask God for things. James 4:2b says, *"Yet ye have not, because you ask not."*

2. You must pray in Jesus name. John 14:13 says, *"And whatsoever ye shall ask in my name, that will I do, that the Father may be glorified in the Son."*

This does not mean that saying the name of Jesus has any magical power in just saying the words. When we pray in Jesus' name it means we are praying according to His will. We should not use the name of Jesus or involve Jesus in things that are not right. By praying in the name of Jesus we are recognizing that we are seeking God's will and are submitting to it.

3. You must pray according to God's will. 1 John 5:14 says, *"And this is the confidence that we have in him, that, if we ask any thing according to his will, he heareth us."* Always want what God wants. Never ask for anything that is sinful or against what the Bible teaches.

4. Stay close to God. John 15:7 says, *"If ye abide (fellowship) in me, and my words abide in you, ye shall ask what ye will, and it shall be done unto you."*

5. Don't ask for selfish reasons. James 4:3 says, *"Ye ask, and receive not, because ye ask amiss, that ye may consume it upon your lusts."* God will not finance our sin by answering selfish prayers.

DON'T FORGET TO PRAY EVERYDAY!

Write out and memorize John 15:7

_____

_____

_____

QUESTIONS:

1. What is prayer?_____.

2. What can we obtain and find at the throne of God? (Heb. 4:16) Obtain _____ and find

_____.

3. What does each letter stand for in the pattern of praying called ACTS?

A_____

C_____

T_____

S_____

4. What does 1John 1:9 tell us about our sin?

_____

_____

_____

5. Name some hindrances to prayer: _____

_____

_____

_____

_____

_____

6. Will you seek to pray every single day? _____

~NOTES~

LESSON

5

What Sin Does To A Christian

Spiritual Death

*"What? Know ye not that
your body is the temple of the
Holy Ghost which is in you,
which ye have of God, and
ye are not your own?
(1 Corinthians 6:19)*

WHAT SIN DOES TO A CHRISTIAN

When we received salvation by trusting in Christ, we became a member of the Body of Christ, the Church. Before our salvation, we served our own desires and Satan's wishes. Now, as a child of God, we have a new relationship with God. We must not take this lightly, because God doesn't take it lightly.

The Bible says in 1Corinthians 6:19-20: "What? *Know ye not that your body is the temple of the Holy Ghost which is in you, which ye have of God, and ye are not your own? For ye are bought with a price: therefore glorify God in your body, and in your spirit, which are God's.*"

Since we are no longer our own, we cannot do as we please. This sounds like we are losing something, doesn't it? It sounds like becoming a Christian means giving up pleasure and joy. Now, we have to be as a slave, losing our freedom of choice and being under bondage to satisfy another. The fact is this; apart from God, we will continue to sin. We will be in the bondage to sin and its destructive influence in our lives. Never forget that SIN is destructive. Look at what sin will cost you:

Jesus said, "*. . . Verily, verily, I say unto you, Whosoever committeth sin is the servant of sin*" (John 8:34). Sin enslaves us.

But this is what the Bible says regarding submitted believers:

"*Being then made free from sin, ye became the servants of righteousness*" (Romans 6:18).

In other words, the Lord sets the believer free from the destructive results of sin. Then, He guides the believer's life toward righteousness. Righteousness means simply doing that which is right and is the opposite of doing that which is wrong.

WHAT ARE THE EFFECTS OF SIN IN A BELIEVER'S LIFE?

1. SIN SEPARATES US FROM THE FELLOWSHIP OF GOD

Isaiah 59:2 "*But your iniquities have separated between you and your God, and your sins have hid his face from you, that he will not hear.*"
The first thing sin does in a Christian's life is to separate us from the fellowship of God. God is holy and will not look upon sin. Our sin causes God to turn His face away. When fellowship is broken we can pray, BUT there is no answer. Psalm 66:18 says, "*If I regard iniquity in my heart, the Lord will not hear me.*"

2. SIN WILL DESTROY THE JOY OF OUR SALVATION

David was a man after God's own heart. He enjoyed the presence of the Lord and God blessed him until sin destroyed that joy. David wept with grief, desiring that joy again. David wrote this in Psalm 51:12, "*Restore unto me the joy of thy salvation; and uphold me with thy free spirit.*"

The second phase of sin in a Christian's life is the loss of joy in their salvation. Such is the case with the loss of joy, which could include but are not limit to the following: loss of joy in going to church, loss of joy in testifying to others about God and the loss of joy in seeing lost souls saved. When this happens, we normally start finding fault with everything and everyone that is godly.

3. SIN WILL BRING THE CHASTENING HAND OF GOD

Hebrews 12:6 reads, *"For whom the Lord loveth he chasteneth, and scourgeth every son whom he receiveth."* Just as a good parent corrects and chastens his disobedient child, God is forced to chasten us because of our disobedience and unwillingness to confess our sin. This chastening may come in different ways. It may be through disappointments, financial loss or trouble upon trouble. Nevertheless, God our Father, must chasten us for sin. Don't ever forget that He does it because He loves us!!

4. SIN CAN BRING PREMATURE DEATH

The most serious state of sin is when God's patience is exhausted and He turns you over to the devil for the destruction of the flesh (not the soul). This can occur when a believer refuses to turn from his sin, and God after much chastening and conviction at His appointed time takes his/her life to stop them from sinning.

1 Corinthians 5:5 *"To deliver such an one unto Satan for the destruction of the flesh, that the spirit may be saved in the day of the Lord Jesus."*
1 John 5:16 *"If any man see his brother sin a sin which is not unto death, he shall ask, and he shall give him life for them that sin not unto death. There is a sin unto death: I do not say that he shall pray for it."*

5. SIN CAUSES GOD TO TAKE AWAY SOME PRECIOUS THINGS

Because of David's sin, God took away someone precious to him, his child that was born out of a sinful relationship.

2 Samuel 12:14 *"Howbeit, because by this deed thou hast given great occasion to the enemies of the LORD to blaspheme, the child also that is born unto thee shall surely die."*

A saved person who turns away from the Lord into sin and refuses to confess and make things right is headed for great sorrow. If necessary, God will take that which is most precious (the distraction) from us in order to bring us back to Him.

6. SIN TAKES AWAY ONES TESTIMONY AND OPPORTUNITY TO GLORIFY THE LORD.

I can truthfully say, I have never seen a husband or wife, who, led their spouse toward receiving Christ who did not live a consistent Christian life. I have never seen a neighbor, relative or friend come to Christ under the influence of a professing Christian who was not actively fighting sin in their own life and living for the Lord. Jesus said, *"Every branch in me that beareth not fruit he taketh away: and every branch that beareth fruit, he purgeth it, that it may bring forth more fruit. . . ., Herein is my Father glorified, that ye bear much fruit; so shall ye be my disciples"* (John 15:2,8).

7. SIN STOPS A CHRISTIAN FROM MATURING

Over my years in ministry I have seen that it is the obedient believer who matures in the Lord. The believer who is obeying the Bible and trying to live by God's Word has trouble just like everyone else. However, the difference is that the maturing believer is able to go through difficult times and not misrepresent the one who has called him or her to salvation. The believer who follows the Word of God is being prepared in advance for the trials that will come their way.

One real hindrance to our overcoming sin is to ignore the problem. Many times we know it is destructive, yet we try to justify it in a number of ways. The most common excuse we use is to plead, "I'm too weak." The fact is you really are, however that excuse doesn't hold water when we read, *"I can do all things through Christ which strengtheneth me"* (Philippians 4:13).

Our pretext to make us feel better is dissolved in the face of Paul's exclamation, *"And ye are complete in him, which is the head of all principality and power"* (Colossians 2:10).

A believer has God's power, *"But as many as received him, to them gave he power to become the sons of God,* (John 1:12). In Christ we can overcome ANYTHING!

Another pretext we use is to say, "I am not really so bad, I don't do really terrible things". Another excuse I've heard was, "I have come a long way from what I was, in time maybe I will overcome this thing also". The real problem with these folks is that they do not accept that - ALL- sin, is sin. God does not give us the latitude to commit any sin. Why? because all sin is destructive. The effect of sin is accumulative. A sin that is allowed to remain will affect your soul.

Think for a moment about why God commands us to turn immediately from all sin. What would you think of a parent who let their child drink alcohol, but would not let them have hard drugs? A foolish parent indeed is one whose thinking is so warped. God wants NO sin in our lives! His standard is righteousness. He wants us never to have to experience the harmful effects of any sin. What kind of God would he be if he overlooked our so called little sins?

Two verses of Scripture puts everything into proper perspective. Carefully read the following verses.

"For whom he did foreknow, he also did predestinate to be conformed to the image of his Son, that he might be the firstborn among many brethren" (Romans 8:29).

"There hath no temptation taken you but such as is common to man: but God is faithful, who will not suffer you to be tempted above that ye are able; but will with the temptation also make a way to escape, that ye may be able to bear it" (1 Corinthians 10:13).

QUESTIONS: There is only one question or assignment for this lesson:

On the next page, in your own words, write down what you think that the previous two verses Romans 8:29 and 1Corinthians 10:13 personally mean to you.

_____

_____

_____

_____

_____

_____

_____

_____

_____

_____

_____

_____

WRITE DOWN ANY QUESTIONS YOU MIGHT HAVE AND PRESENT THEM TO YOUR PASTOR OR TEACHER OF THIS LESSON!

_____

_____

_____

_____

_____

_____

~NOTES~

LESSON

6

Let's Learn Doctrine

Teaching

*"Till I come,
give attendance
to reading,
to exhortation,
to doctrine."*
(1 Timothy 4:13)

LET'S LEARN DOCTRINE

Paul had much to say about doctrine and its importance. Doctrine is simply the teachings of the Bible, God's Word. As Christians, we should know what the Bible teaches. Please have your Bible with you as you read this chapter. This chapter is to help you to use your Bible more often. Paul told Timothy in 1 Timothy 4:13, *"Till I come, give attendance to reading, to exhortation, to doctrine."* In 2 Timothy 3:16 says, ***"All scripture is given by inspiration of God, and is profitable for doctrine, for reproof, for correction, for instruction in righteousness: That the man of God may be perfect, throughly furnished unto all good works."***

LET'S LEARN SOME DOCTRINES:

1. DOCTRINE OF THE BIBLE

We believe in the Bible as the inspired Word of God (every word inspired and completely given to us), as we find in the original manuscripts. All portions of scripture are equally inspired and contain no contradictions. The 66 books we have, complete the Bible, never to be added to or taken from.
Reference Text: 1 Timothy 3:16; Hebrews 1:1; 2 Peter 1:18-21; Revelations 22:18-19.

2. DOCTRINE OF GOD

We believe the Godhead exists in three persons - God the Father, God the Son, and God the Holy Spirit. They are eternal. These three make one God, which is called the Trinity. They are equal in all respects.
Reference Text: Genesis 1:1, 1:25; John 1:1, 14; John 14:16-17; 1 Timothy 3:16.

3. DOCTRINE OF JESUS CHRIST

We believe that Jesus is God the Son (deity), born of a virgin and begotten by the Holy Spirit. He was God and man - the God-Man. He is the only way to receive salvation. He died, was buried, and rose again the third day. He is coming back for us, the church. He was without any sin whatsoever.
Reference Text: Isaiah 7:14; Luke 1:35; 1 John 1:1-4; John 10:30; John 14:6; 1 Timothy 2:5-6; 1 Thessalonians 4:13-18; Revelation 20:4-6.

4. DOCTRINE OF THE HOLY SPIRIT

We believe the Holy Spirit is God and equal with the Father and Son. He is a person, not just an influence. He convicts, regenerates, indwells, seals, infill's, empowers and guides the believer. When you got saved the Holy Spirit came into your heart.
Reference Text: John 16:7-13; Acts 1:8; 1 Corinthians 6:19; Ephesians 1:13; 5:18.

5. DOCTRINE OF MAN

We believe that God created man in His own image and that man sinned against God. All men are born with a sinful nature, and must be born again or he will be eternally lost in hell.
Reference Text: Genesis 1:26-27; Psalm 51:5; Romans 3:23; Revelation 20:11-15; Revelation 21:8.

6. DOCTRINE OF SALVATION

We believe a person is saved when he repents of his sin and turns in faith by accepting Jesus Christ as his personal Savior. The believer is kept by the power of God and is eternally secure in Christ.

Salvation includes access to the forgiveness of sins past, present, and future. It gives us right standing before God in Jesus Christ.

Death fixes the fate of a person, no second chance after death.

Reference Text: John 1:12; John 5:24; John 10:28, 29; 1 Peter 1:5; Ephesians 2:8-10; Hebrews 9:27; Revelation 20:11-15.

7. DOCTRINE OF THE CHURCH

We believe the local church is:

a. Composed of members of the Body of Christ who are Spirit-governed, and who make up the universal Body of Christ.

b. Composed of believers baptized in the Body of Christ.

c. Composed of believers who are organized and have ministry gifts in operation such as Apostle, Prophet, Evangelist, Pastor and Teacher, Helps, etc.

d. Composed of believers who meet regularly for fellowship, worship and Bible study.

e. Composed of believers who observe ordinances of Baptism and the Lord's Supper.

f. Composed of believers who carry out The Great Commission.

Reference Text: 1 Corinthians 12:13; Acts 2:41, 47; Hebrews 10:35; 1 Corinthians 11:23; Matthew 28:18-20.

8. DOCTRINE OF SATAN AND FALLEN ANGELS

We believe that Satan is a personal being, who was created perfectly by God. But when he chose to sin and became the arch enemy of God and His creation. He is the believers chief adversary. He seeks to keep men from Christ and believers from living for the Lord. He is in command of a host of fallen angels (demons) who carry out his orders. He has only the power God allows him, and will one day be cast into the lake of fire forever.

Reference Text: Ezekiel 28:12-19; Isaiah 14:12-15; Revelation 12:10; Revelation 20:10.

Write out and memorize 2 Timothy 3:16

_____

_____

_____

_____

~NOTES~

_____

_____

_____

_____

_____

_____

_____

_____

_____

_____

_____

_____

_____

_____

_____

LESSON

7

You Should Be A Soul Winner

Witnessing

*"But you shall receive power,
after that the Holy Ghost is come upon you:
and ye shall be witnesses unto me both
in Jerusalem, and in all Ju-dae´-a, and
in Sa-ma´-ri-a, and the uttermost part
of the earth."*
(Acts 1:8)

YOU SHOULD BE A SOUL-WINNER

Proverbs 11:30: "*. . . he that winneth souls is wise*".

2 Timothy 2:2: "*And the things that thou hast heard of me among many witnesses, the same commit thou to faithful men, who shall be able to teach others also.*"

We have a responsibility to pass on to others what we have received. We have received Christ and His salvation. We should tell others of Christ and the way of salvation. Mark 16:15 tells us to, "*go into all the world and preach the gospel to every creature.*" Every Christian can and should witness for Jesus Christ. Jesus also promised us that when the Holy Spirit came He would give us power to be witnesses for Christ (Acts 1:8).
A witness is simply one who tells what he has heard, seen and experienced.

WHAT CAN I DO TO BE A SOUL WINNER?

A. If I have obeyed the gospel, I can at least tell others what I have done. Mark 5:19-20
B. I can study and grow in my knowledge of God so that in time I will be a capable teacher. 2 Tim. 2:15
C. I can invite others to services where they will hear the gospel. Romans 10:14
D. I can make an effort to attend Bible studies. Hebrews 10:25
E. I can join my church outreach ministry. Matthews 28:19-20
F. I can get some Gospel tracts and pass them out. Gospel tracts are mini booklets or pamphlets like Chick tracts which are available at Christian bookstores and from Chick Publications. You may also get some from Fellowship Tract League and Tract Plant.com to name a few. Your local church may also supply tracts.

IS IT IMPORTANT?

The work of winning souls is the greatest job on this earth. The eternal souls of men, women, and children depend upon our telling them. If we don't tell them of Christ and His desire to save them, they will perish in hell forever. Therefore, let's consider the A B C's of soul- winning.

1. APPEARANCE (A)

Many would not think this to be important, but it is. You are displaying God to the lost. The unsaved person has many ideas about Christians, so we should be the best representatives of Christ we can. Don't forget, the neighbors are watching the appearance of you, your family, your yard, and even how you keep your house. Be a good example. Our life is the greatest witness or testimony to others.

2. BEHAVIOR (B)

Always be nice to people, regardless of the circumstances in which you might find yourself. Try to win the persons confidence and friendship (when possible) even before witnessing to him. Talk about things that will arrest their interest. Remember how you behave has a direct impact on whether people observing you will take you serious.

3. COMPASSION (C)

This may be the most important of the three. Always be mindful that when you witness to a person, he or she will live forever either in heaven or in hell. Before you begin your day, be sure to pray and ask God to help you.
The Holy Spirit will guide and help you in witnessing. We never go alone, for He is with us always.

ONCE A PERSON EXPRESSES A DESIRE TO HEAR ABOUT THE GOSPEL

After a casual conversation, you might begin to witness by asking a question like this. "May I ask you a question? If you were to die today, would you know if you would go to heaven?" Unless they are saved, they will usually reply, "I hope so," "I don't know," "No," etc. Then you might say this, "Do you mind if I show you from the Bible how you can be saved and know it?" Most people will allow you to do it. Now is when you open your New Testament (use a small Bible). Try to let the person you are talking with see what you are reading. Ask if they have a Bible, and let them look up the references with you.

SUGGESTIVE VERSES TO SHARE WITH THEM

You would then start with Romans 3:23, and read aloud to them, *"For all have sinned, and come short of the glory of God."* Be sure to include yourself when explaining how all have sinned. Regardless of how good or bad we are we have all been sinners until we choose to accept Christ as Lord and Saviour.

Read to him or her Romans 6:23, *"For the wages of sin is death; but the gift of God is eternal life through Jesus Christ our Lord."* Explain that sin pays wages, death, but that God gives a gift, which is life through Christ.

Then read to him or her Romans 5:8, *"But God commendeth his love toward us, in that, while we were yet sinners, Christ died for us."* Even though we are sinners and deserve to go to hell, Jesus died for us so we could be saved. He died in our place as our substitute. He shed His blood for us to wash away our sins. Christ is the only answer and hope to a persons needs.

Then tell him or her what God desires them to do, read to them Romans 10:9, 13, *"That if thou shalt confess with thy mouth the Lord Jesus, and shalt believe in thine heart that God hath raised him from the dead, thou shalt be saved... For whosoever shall call upon the name of the Lord shall be saved."* We must believe that Jesus died for us, was buried and arose from the dead after three days. God will do what He has promised, for God cannot lie.

Make sure he or she realizes that they are sinners and deserve hell, but Jesus died for them. As a result, he or she must call upon God for salvation and confess Jesus as their Lord and Savior to receive eternal life. Encourage the person to pray for salvation, but don't try to force the individual.

Rejoice with the person after they pray. Give him or her the assurance that God did save them, because God cannot lie. You should read a few verses from the Bible to show that they can know they are saved. (for these, see Lesson #1, The New Life) Invite them to come to church with you to the very next service. Encourage him or her to share their salvation experience with others.

Every Christian should and can be a soul-winner. Witness in your neighborhood, to your family, co-workers, or whenever God opens a door. The only link that God has between His Word and the sinners are Christians like you and I. By the same token, the only opportunity many will have to be saved is if you and I tell them about God's plan for saving man.

Write and memorize Acts 1:8

_____

_____

_____

_____

1. Which is probably the most important of the ABC's of soul winning to you and why? _____

_____

_____

_____

_____

2. What is the first thing a person should realize about himself before he can be saved? (Romans 3:23)

_____

3. What are we to confess in order to be saved? (Romans 10:9)?

_____

_____

4. Have you witnessed to someone since you have been saved? _____

CONCLUSION: *The only link that God has between His Word and the sinners are Christians like you and I. By the same token, the only opportunity many will have to be saved is if you and I tell them about God's plan for saving man.*

~NOTES~

~NOTES~

BONUS CHAPTER

As Christians we are to feed our spirit not our flesh.
Everything that we hear or see has a direct impact on our lives.
With that in mind I want to share some information
on the areas of entertainment and music.

Guidelines To Consider for Entertainment

1. What are some biblical principles that will help guide my entertainment choices?

A. Beware of anything that makes you calloused to sin or lessens your hatred of evil.

Paul warns us several times in the New Testament to *"hate what is evil"* and *"avoid every kind of evil"* (Romans 12:9; 1 Thessalonians 5:22). He repeats this command because the world surrounds us with all sorts of evil and perversion. As humans, our natural tendency is to "get used to" whatever we consistently encounter in our environment. The enemy knows this and tries to make us as calloused to sin as he can.

A writer once wrote, ***"Vice is a monster of so frightful mien, As to be hated needs but to be seen; Yet seen too oft, familiar with her face, We first endure, then pity, then embrace."***

In other words, it is difficult to hate what you are used to.

It's not hard to discern when a movie or book has too much violence or cursing. Nonetheless, are you also noticing when your entertainment choice is pushing a worldly philosophy or value system? Ungodly attitudes and belief systems can be as damaging to our minds as the more obvious sensual allurements.

B. Beware of anything that bothers your conscience.

In his first letter to Timothy, Paul urged him to hold on to *"faith and a good conscience, which some having put away concerning faith have made shipwreck"* (1 Timothy 1:18,19). Paul also told the Romans *"whatsoever is not of faith is sin"* (Romans 14:22,23). The main thrust of Paul's message is that we shouldn't do anything that we believe is wrong. This principle clearly applies to those "gray areas" of life which are not specifically mentioned in Scripture. We need to be sensitive to the prompting of the Holy Spirit, and respond in obedience when we feel a check about a certain activity or form of entertainment. Keep your conscience clear!

C. Beware of anything that would make another believer stumble.

Romans 14 is a thought provoking chapter on the impact that our actions have on other brothers and sisters. Paul says, *"let us not judge one another anymore, but judge (or determine) this rather, that no man put a stumbling block or an occasion to fall in his brother's way"* (Romans 14:13). He also says, *"It is good not to eat meat or to drink wine, or to do anything by which your brother stumbles"* (Romans 14:21). This is an important factor that should be taken into account when we participate in various kinds of entertainment.

We need to be sensitive to the concerns and weaknesses of those around us. There are times when it is necessary to limit our own desires in deference to someone else. Don't be irritated or frustrated with them—be kind and remember that one day, someone may have to be sensitive to you. Note: Pastors after God's own heart, are constantly limiting their own desires and pleasures because of what people might think.

D. Beware of anything that appeals to or affects your areas of weakness.

We all have areas of weakness and most of us know what they are. Unfortunately, the enemy knows them too, and the temptations we face are always tailored for a perfect fit. James, the Lord's brother, said, *"But each one is tempted when he is drawn away by his own desires and enticed"* (James 1:14).
Entertainment, probably more than anything else, has the ability to appeal to our areas of weakness. Because of this, it is imperative that we filter our activities through the grid of what is spiritually healthy for us. Know your weaknesses and don't let enemy trap you!

E. Beware of anything that portrays sin as amusing or glorifies evil.

Paul urged the Romans to stop being *"conformed to this world, but be transformed by the renewing of your mind"* (Romans 12:2). The world is constantly trying to squeeze us into its mold, and one of its most effective tools is sugarcoated sin. How many of us have read a book or watched a movie where the rebellious attitudes of the hero are presented as funny? Often disrespect for authority is portrayed as cool and immorality is shown as comical. There are even TV shows that glorify witchcraft and homosexuality. It's important that we avoid this kind of entertainment because the enemy will use it to influence and shape our perspective of sin. God doesn't think sin is funny—to Him its deadly serious.

F. Beware of anything that stimulates wrong thoughts or attitudes.

At first glance this principle seems impossible to put into practice. After all, we're surrounded by the world's pollution everywhere we go. But the fact that the enemy is peddling his perversion in the streets is no reason to invite him into your home. In his letter to the Philippians, Paul told them *"whatever things are true, whatever things are honest, whatever things are just, whatever things are pure, whatever things are lovely, whatever things are of good report, if there be any virtue, and if there be praise, think on these things"* (Philippians 4:8).

The various ways we choose to entertain ourselves should pass the test of this verse. Remember, God isn't trying to prevent us from enjoying life. He's trying to protect us from activities that will stimulate wrong thoughts or attitudes. Sin begins in the mind—avoid anything that gives it a chance to get started or grow.

G. Beware of loving pleasure more than loving God.

In his last letter to Timothy, Paul warned him that in the last days difficult times would come. *"For men shall be...lovers of pleasure more than lovers of God"* (2 Timothy 3:4). Now it is easier to fall into this trap than most people think. Entertainment, even in its most wholesome form, can be used by the enemy to take God's rightful place of supremacy in our lives. A hobby or sport can gradually take up more and more time in our busy schedules until it squeezes out our time with God. Some of our favorite activities can become idols if we allow them to be more important to us than God. God has given us so much to enjoy. Let's make sure we don't worship the creation more than the creator.

A good test of whether or not a certain type of entertainment has become too important in your life is to ask yourself this question: If God were to tell you to stop doing that particular activity, would you welcome His guidance with gratitude, or would you resent His command as an intrusion?

A somewhat innocent pleasure that people often overlook is going to church. Going to church becomes a form of pleasure or entertainment when our reason for going is not to worship God and grow in Christ. Some people have many reasons for attending church. Whatever, your reason is for going is between you and God.

H. Beware of the company you keep.

1. What you do to entertain yourself is often determined by who you spend your time with.
Paul tells us in 1 Corinthians 15:33 – *"Be not deceived: 'evil communications (from bad company) corrupt good manners'."* You need to be careful who you decide to associate with.

2. What is the role of the man/husband when it comes to entertainment?
   a. The man sets the direction in the home (or relationship) when it comes to entertainment. This is an important responsibility and should not be taken lightly.
   b. The man sets the example for his wife and children. They are watching how you entertain yourself. Remember that what you allow in moderation, your children will often excuse in excess.
   c. Children should not be allowed to make their own choices when it comes to entertainment. They do not have the experience and discernment to make godly decisions. You, as the parent, should control how they entertain themselves. My advice is that you pray for God's directions when it come to allowing your children to have their own TVs, radios, ipods, ipads, cell-phones (they can surf the web) or computers. What they watch and listen to should be done in such a way that you can supervise and control it.

3. What is the role of the wife/single woman when it comes to entertainment?
As wife and mother or just a mother, you have control over most of your children's entertainment choices. Be aware of the books they read, the music they listen to and the movies they watch. It is a good idea that you pre-view whatever they will have access to in the way of entertainment. Make sure that it supports your value systems and promotes godliness.

4. A lot has been mentioned about what I should avoid when it comes to entertainment.
   Now let's look at some things that I should pursue.
   a. Pursue fellowship with other believers. Getting together with other Christians and playing bible -trivia type board games is a great way to have fellowship in a edifying environment.
   b. Pursue Christian movies. More and more movies are being made by and for Christians. "Last Ounce Of Courage" and "God Is Not Dead" are two such movies that I have recently enjoyed. Feature Films for Families also have many good choices available.
   c. Pursue Christian books. There are many good choices available at Christian bookstores.
   d. Pursue Christian websites. Surfing the web can be fun, but it is also dangerous. Seek out Christ-centered websites. There are lots of them out there. Your church website as well as other Christian websites.
   e. Pursue Christian radio and music stations.

Things To Keep In Mind About Music

The apostle Paul mentions music in his letters to the Colossians and the Ephesians:

Colossians 3:16 – *"Let the word of Christ dwell in you richly in all wisdom; teaching and admonishing one another in psalms and hymns and spiritual songs, singing with grace in your hearts to the Lord."*

Ephesians 5:18-20 – *"And be not drunk with wine, wherein is excess; but be filled with the Spirit: Speaking to yourself in psalms and hymns and spiritual songs, singing and making melody with your heart to the Lord; Giving thanks always for all things unto God and the Father in the name of our Lord Jesus Christ."*

Here are some principles I believe we can derive from these verses:

a. Music and singing are associated with an attitude of thankfulness and gratitude toward God. Are you paying attention to the attitudes the music you listen to encourage you to have?

b. Music is an activity that you are encouraged to do with other believers. It has the unique ability to unite a group of individuals into a single unit (the essence of harmony).

c. Music and lyrics are closely connected. Some music, like rap, has lyrics that are obviously vulgar and ungodly. Yet other kinds of music can have more subtle lyric issues: bad values, beliefs, attitudes, etc. If you are listening to Christian music, do the lyrics exalt God or focus on self? If you are listening to secular music, do the values expressed glorify God? Even music that is not about God or Christian living should be in harmony with what is right and true. (This is not an endorsement of any secular music)

d. Music can exert a controlling influence over your mind. The music you listen to should be in harmony with the truth, or you risk giving yourself over to something that is not of the Holy Spirit. You can listen to music that creates desires for romance, passion and sex to name a few. Does the music you listen to cause you to have godly or ungodly desires?

e. Music is associated with edification and the uplifting of the heart and mind. Does the music you listen to encourage you or depress you? Does it create a spirit of discontentment or a spirit of hope and joy?

f. Music prompts a physical response in the listener. Some music can put you to sleep and other music can make you want to sing and dance. Be sensitive to what the music is prompting you to do with your body.

g. Music expresses emotion. Certain kinds of music are designed to channel anger and frustration (e.g. rock music was/is designed to help block out feelings of guilt). Other kinds of music express peace and happiness. Be aware of the kinds of emotions that the music you listen to is creating.

h. Music is associated with the performer. How many teenager's rooms have posters on the wall of their favorite music groups? People naturally admire the performers of the music styles they enjoy. Are the performers you listen to living godly lives? Are their lifestyles worth imitating or would they lead you astray?

A WORD TO NEW BELIEVERS

Make it up in your mind to avoid any music that reminds you of what you used to listen to as a sinner. Music often goes hand-in-hand with drinking, smoking and partying in the world. I have found that music can often lead people back into their old habits and lifestyles (there are exceptions to this rule, but it is a good rule of thumb).

_____

_____

_____

_____

_____

_____

_____

_____

_____

_____

_____

_____

_____

_____

_____

_____

_____

_____

~NOTES~